A. ALVAREZ, born in London in 1929, was educated at Oundle and Oxford. Out of research and teaching in Oxford and America came a critical study of modern poetry, *The Shaping Spirit* (1958). Since 1956, when not travelling or making academic forays to the United States (most recently as a Visiting Professor at the State University of New York, Buffalo), he has lived as a freelance writer in London. His seminars on criticism at Princeton University in 1958 resulted in another book, *The School of Donne* (1961). Alvarez is Poetry Editor with the *Observer*. In 1961 he received the Vachel Lindsay Prize from *Poetry* (Chicago). He has edited *The New Poetry* for Penguin Books, and written, among other works, *Under Pressure* (1965) and *Beyond All This Fiddle* (1968).

ROY FULLER was born in Lancashire in 1912. He qualified as a solicitor in 1933 and practised until 1969, for the most part with the Woolwich Equitable Building Society, of which he is now a director. His first collection of poetry was published in 1939 and his *Collected Poems* in 1962. Since the latter, there have been two further volumes of poetry, the latest, *New Poems*, being awarded the Duff Cooper Memorial Prize. He is also a novelist and currently Professor of Poetry in the University of Oxford.

ANTHONY THWAITE was born in 1930 and, after military service in Libya, read English at Oxford. He married Anne Thwaite, also a writer, and spent two years lecturing in English literature at Tokyo University. He was a BBC producer and literary editor of the *Listener* before moving to Benghazi with his family and teaching English at the University of Libya. Just after the Arab–Israeli war of 1967 they returned to England, and Thwaite became literary editor of the *New Statesman*. His own publications include three books of poems and a short critical book. With Geoffrey Bownas he edited *The Penguin Book of Japanese Verse*.

Penguin Modern Poets

18

A. ALVAREZ

ROY FULLER

ANTHONY THWAITE

Penguin Books

Penguin Books Ltd, Harmondsworth, Middlesex, England
Penguin Books Inc., 7110 Ambassador Road, Baltimore, Maryland 21207, U.S.A.
Penguin Books Australia Ltd, Ringwood, Victoria, Australia

—

This selection first published 1970

—

Copyright © Penguin Books Ltd, 1970

—

Made and printed in Great Britain
by C. Nicholls & Company Ltd
Set in Monotype Garamond

Contents

CONTENTS

CONTENTS

Acknowledgements

Some of the poems by A. Alvarez were first published in *The End of It*, 1958, privately printed, *Lost*, Turret Press, 1968 and 12 *Poems*, The Review, 1968.

For the poems by Roy Fuller from *Collected Poems 1936–61*, *Buff* and *New Poems*, grateful acknowledgement is made to André Deutsch Ltd, and to the author for unpublished poems.

For the poems by Anthony Thwaite from *The Owl in The Tree: Poems*, 1963, and *The Stones of Emptiness: Poems 1963–6*, 1967, grateful acknowledgement is made to the Oxford University Press, and to the author for unpublished poems.

A. ALVAREZ

I

Mourning and Melancholia

His face was blue, on his fingers
Flecks of green. 'This is my father',
I thought. Stiff and unwieldy
He stared out of my sleep. The parlourmaid
Smiled from the bed with his corpse,
Her chapped lips thin and welcoming.
In the next room her albino child
Kept shouting, shouting. I had to put him down
Like a blind puppy. 'Death from strangulation
By persons known.' I kept the clipping
In my breast-pocket where it burns and burns,
Stuck to my skin like phosphorus.

I wake up struggling, silent, undersea
Light and a single thrush
Is tuning up. You sleep, the baby sleeps,
The town is dead. Foxes are out on the Heath;
They sniff the air like knives.
A hawk turns slowly over Highgate, waiting.
This is the hidden life of London. Wild.

Three years back my father's corpse was burnt,
His ashes scattered. Now I breathe him in
With the grey morning air, in and out.
In out. My heart bumps steadily
Without pleasure. The air is thick with ash.
In out. I am cold and powerless. His face
Still pushes sadly into mine. He's disappointed.
I've let him down, he says. Now I'm cold like him.
Cold and untameable. Will have to be put down.

1968

Coming Back

Finer and clearer than the mountain air
Or the wheeling New Mexican sun.
Your scent in the back of my mind like a cry from another
    street.
Something uncoils and breathes. Night moves
With the musky taste of summer. Turn and sleep.
Your eyes change in the firelight. You have changed.

Love, the weather has turned, the swallows are back
And I wake in your scattered hair sensing rain
Where the trees arch over our bed.
Their thin leaves rustle your name.

1969

The Killing

It caught him by the throat, threw him down,
Teeth working like machines. He stared
Up at the thing and waited. Was death like this?
A dark stain spread across the heart
He raised to shield himself. It hung there ripped
But still beating. 'This maniac
Eats human flesh', he thought. 'God is a cannibal.'
A single blade of fear opened his chest.
Aloud he said, 'How can he bear the taste?'
His mind flickered against the light,
Face twisted away, eyes shut tight.

Then lay exhausted, watching the watery shadows
Run on the ceiling. Nothing moved outside
Except the leaves plotting together. In street
After street bodies were junked like cars.
His heavy spirit moved among the derelicts
Sex had smashed up, until a far-off clock
Struck four. A single blackbird cleared its throat,
The bristling shadows thinned. Death could wait.

1969

War Stories

The first time they all looked shocked.
'Don't tell such filthy stories
around here', they said. 'How dare you?'
And everyone snickered.

The second time they shook a little
and there was a booming
something like laughter. As the dust rose
he found himself crying.

The third time he brought the house down.
They rolled in the aisles and the aisles rolled.
'That's marvellous', they cried, tears streaming down their
   faces,
'O, do stop'. And blew him to pieces.

1963

Operation

The town froze, close as a fist.
Winter was setting about us.
Like birds the bare trees shivered,
Birds without leaves or nests
As the fog took over.

My words were all gone, my tongue sour.
We sat in the car like the dead
Awaiting the dead. Your hair
Wept round your face like a willow
Unstirring. Your eyes were dry.

Unbodied, like smoke in the crowd,
You vanished. Later came violence.
Not that you felt it or cared,
Swaddled in drugs, apart
In some fractured, offensive dream,
While a bog-Irish nurse mopped up.

'Leave me. I'm bleeding. I bleed
Still. But he didn't hurt me'.
Pale as the dead. As the dead
Fragile. Vague as the city
Now the fog chokes down again.
A life was pitched out like garbage.

'I'm bleeding. A boy, they said'.
My blood stings like a river
Lurching over the falls.
My hands are bloody. My mind
Is rinsed with it. Blood fails me.

You lie like the dead, still bleeding,
While his fingers, unformed, unerring,
Hold us and pick us to pieces.

1962

Apparition

'Beaver. Beaver', you whisper,
'Beaver', yearningly.
A wetness glimmers,
Sleek fur, teeth sly,
Cold paw at your throat,
Cold eye to your eye
Cold cold cold.
'Help me', you sigh,
Shoulder bloody, breasts straining
To the shuddering, stained sky.

1963

Back

The night I came back from the hospital, scarcely
Knowing what had happened or when,
I went through the whole performance again in my dreams.
Three times – in a dance, in a chase and in something
Now lost – my body was seized and shaken
Till my jaw swung loose, my eyes were almost out
And my trunk was stunned and stretched with a vibration
Sharper than fear, closer than pain. It was death.
So I sweated under the sheets, afraid to sleep,
Though you breathed all night quietly enough by my side.

Was it the *tremor mortis*, the last dissolution
Known now in dreams, unknown in the pit itself
When I was gripped by the neck till my life shook
Like loosening teeth in my head? Yet I recall
Nothing of death but the puzzled look on your face,
Swimming towards me, weeping, clouded, uncertain,
As they took the tube from my arm
And plugged the strange world back in place.

1961

Lovers

Eres como la rosa
De Alejandria:
Colorada la noche,
Blanca de día.

White by day coloured by night
Vivid watching changing white
As lightning by day by night
Seeping colours corrupting cheek wrist hand
As blood runs as fire trembles as green
Water flickers or a bland
Glass block shatters rainbows between
My eye and the fused sunlight

By night coloured by day white

1962

Spring Fever

Too young to know
And far too young to care
What shapes hover
At the head of the stair

You twist your hands,
Your hair falls round your face
Darkly. The fire breeds shadows.
I keep my place

Although the rain wakes
And the blackbirds call
Fluently, fluently
The leaves uncurl

On wet apple trees.
You stretch your arms
Pleased with your body's
Fluent warmth.
But your eyes stay down.

Be wakeful. Be gentle.
Look, the dark gathers
Inside your head.
It tangles your fingers.
Your wrists fill with blood.

Be gentle. Be wakeful.
From the fire to the shadows
At the top of the stairs
Come to bed.

1962

Lost

My sleep falters and the good dreams:
The sky lit green, you reaching, reaching out
Through a bell of air. I stir.

The same wrist lies along my cheek;
My fingers touch it. The same head on my chest
Stirs. My arms round the same body;
And I feel the dead arms stir.
My fingers in the same dead hair.
The same belly, dead thighs stir.

The dream whirrs, cuts. The day blinks, stirs.
Hers. Not yours, my love. Hers.

1961

II

The Gate

I knew she stood at the gate
And I should swing over towards her
And open the gate on the flood
And the field running down to the water.

But I couldn't. The water ran on,
She went about her work
Wistful, puzzled, dark.
When I opened the gate she had gone.

The fields have dried out and the sun
Has shattered their surface like glass.
Splintered, silvered, down
Lies the gate I couldn't cross.

'Come to me later, elsewhere',
Like rain her voice sighs in the pines,
'Elk range our pastures here,
Bob-cat, bear and porcupine'.

1959

Love Affair

The sun sees many flowers, but the flower sees only the sun:
Blinded three parts of the day, or dark all dark,
Uneasy, cold, attentive for release,
He crouches through the night, or burns and swells
Blindly as in a kind of hurt of love.
They call it blossoming. The unwieldy earth
Clamps round, his sap distrained and petals shrunk.

And nothing is said. The sun moves on above
Indifferent, raging in its own sweet fire
And light, light, light, the flower twists for it,
Straining its mouth for death, which it calls love.
'A god has come upon me', gapes the flower
As over the lip of the earth the sun sinks down.
The moon swings to and fro between the trees
Its casual, icy face. The first leaves fall.

1960

The Nativity in New Mexico

Heaving, as though nailed down, and weak with fear
She lay staring at the window pane,
Past vacant yard, past ponderoso, where
The desert rolled beneath the mounting sun.

Moaned and turned over. Through the empty air
Sent out her breath towards the breathless plain
In one long, sliding, fading heave of terror.
She heard her husband stir in the next room.

Let him. The blank wind moved across the yard,
The needles of the pine lifted and fell
Against the fiery morning. And she heard
Out of the fire the grating voices call.

So. So. Now her time has passed she strains to see
The grinning midwife lift on high, heels first,
The child, inverted, crying gratingly.
Her thighs are sticky with the afterbirth.

1958

Night Music

It started as a sound deep in your throat,
Gutteral, needy, blind as though with pain,
A song not sung for me. You sing yourself:
A voice thrown over voices, a wish calling
Out of the body's pit, till the god emerges
Unhurried. Dark behind him floats his hair.

He moves as wave on wave; between them, stillness.
Infirm as water, steady as the tide
Your voice runs too and sleep runs underneath.

The god of the house stands at the foot of our bed,
A thickening of darkness against the unsteady shadows,
And makes no sign. He would not stir a feather
Although the wind runs wild in the trees outside.

So, as I sleep, you watch. You change my dreams
With weeping in the dark till sleep becomes
Uneasy, dry and eerie as your song.

1960

Anger

They go at each other like wolves hunting in winter
In a land made thin and savage by the cold.
Is it the season sets one at the other,
    Where once the forest was love?

Is it the season edges them together
Violent and raw as nerves? Now tooth and pelt
Rasp into life as flint upon a tinder,
    Yet once the substance was love.

Now they have done with sidling from thicket to thicket,
The forest knots like a storm about their heads
And a wind poises evilly in the blackness
    Which once was easy with love.

They twist apart, stopped short by their hearts' thick violence.
The starved, hard, anguished landscape lets them in,
Two dwindling backs gone grey and thin with distance
    Where once was the forest of love.

1957

Waking

A train was crying as the dawn came up
Uncanny, unreal, greyish. The birds began,
Before the humans the birds were harshly twittering,
Crying on all sides, rustling and peopling the air
With outcry, like a river suddenly heard,
A heavy, persistent down-calling. So the birds
Were shaking their song out, wrenching and spilling it
Out of the roots of the heart painfully singing.

Out of the roots of the heart painfully twisting
The cold comes blank as the dawn over our bed
Where you lie with your body away, your face to the wall.
Should I get up, go out and leave you asleep
Before the business of the day has taken us,
Creak down the stairs and out? But to what purpose?
The birds will lose their song in the dull street,
The lorries roll and life goes out of us.

Dying. With so much hate behind the tongue,
The nerves grate but the mouth rests surly and slow,
And action turns on itself. A door bangs shut
And God knows now who in the shadow lurks.
My stomach twists to see your passive hands,
Your tensed and quiet forehead, beating throat.
But much good it would do to be up and quit of the lot.

For the beautiful summer is lost and lost the birds,
The lucid, moving air, the swaying elms
And all the confusing paraphernalia of love.
We are left to ourselves in our grey untender rooms,
Sleeping the nights apart in the same bed,

Divided by fears and loss and ignorance.
The dawn comes up and the birds sing to themselves.

1959

Autumn Marriage

Wife: The year is moving out and I too turn
     To noise and colour . . .

Husband: Fictions. Here at home
     Marriage breeds silence round us and between.

Wife: There's something else I need, something you lack
     To split my fabric open to the heart.

Husband: 'They have it very oft that have it not.'

Wife: Domestic weather, violent and void,
     Clouds us from the kitchen to the bed.

Husband: Who would have dreamed the sky could turn so
        black?

Wife: This summer sickens me, this harvest calm
     Without fruition strips me to the bone.
     My heart curls like a leaf, my sap is down.

Husband: Then wait for the colder season, glassy dawns,
     Frost shapes on the window, rime on the lawn,
     The birds piping chill from the gun-blue stones.
     Then, despite blankets, hot water-bottle, stove,
     The heart contracts its kingdom and you'll move
     Back toward me for warmth . . .

Wife: If not for love.

1959

The Hunt

The air is dry as salt, the desert ribbed
Between scrub and heat and mountain.
The sun bakes like an eye in a blank face,
Or, delicate as a mother, swells the moon.

By night the stars are touchable as fruit
About the hut; the undergrowth is quick
With hidden life. Deer tread the cooling fields
Like ghosts, and shrill as ghosts the swaying bats.

And so I hunt by night. I see with my feet
Among the piñon, along vague, straggling tracks
Up from the cabin, through the breathing forest,
Moving by moonlight. Silent. Silence. Stealth.

A tentative sound begins: a woman talking
Raptly, excitedly murmuring to herself?
The mountain stream runs thin as breath through its shallows.
I follow the woman's voice to its dammed-up source

Where logs are tangled thick and silt builds up,
Where water flickers fragile and loose as light
And something hesitates: a shadow drinks at the clearness,
Insubstantial, takes substance like food from a cup.

I gather, silent and poised among the bushes.
(Life of my life, flesh of my flesh) I aim
And (with my body I thee worship) fire.
The creature rises, arches, flays the pool.

31

Its legs as taut as needles, its head wild.
It leaps like a cry on the air, is torn inside
And gives out its life to the watery silt and the moon.
Shapeless. Jerking. Loveless. Without pride.

Slowly the noise dies away. The heart's crashing
Fades up the mountain and settles, too, the shocked
Whisper and rustle of beasts who have seen the slaying.
The creature trembles. It is my own blood spurts.

1960

Sunstruck

My eyes swayed, I curved
As though kicked in the groin.
And you were full of it, thick with the sun.
In your delicate, reeking skin,
Swollen, tasting of brine,
Those shuttered afternoons:
Feet bare on the tiles, the muffled sounds
Outside and muffled, hissing within
The rustle of love. Light in bars. A thin
Crying. High up. Held up. Sliding. Sliding. Gone.
You came back full of it,
Wanting another man's child.
Sick to the bone, the vein, the groin.
Thick with the sun.

1962

The Picture Gallery

The voices fade and steps, as dry as air . . .
Where do you lie now? Under what shifting trees?
Under whose shifting hands? . . . Startled the images
As rain drifts round the eaves,
Each in his own gold frame. Pain hangs on the walls,
Sifts like dust from the palms
While the spiked head, watching, lolls.

Even the mother and child are tense with waiting;
They stare from the wall with the same aching eyes.

The mother twines with the child. The frame empties . . .
Under whose hands you lie, under whose . . . Streets
Flicker with lights, with fragments twisted together . . .
Thrusting, the hands with hands twine, feet with feet . . .

Pain in the brick, in asphalt as in marble,
Turning the earth in spring as a heel grinds down,
Wrenches the vivid beak of a whistling blackbird
Whose eye is sharp as a knife among the leaves,
Hovers, pounces, tears, and does not breed . . .
You lie against him listlessly for hours;
Your breathing is an ache, your sex a bruise . . .

It wakes with the restless child turning at midnight,
Leans at the foot of the bed attentive at dawn . . .
Who stirs? Who moves a hand along your spine? . . .
Starts from the lights as traffic nudges forward,
Sways through the park where lovers flicker and weave . . .
And in your mouth whispers obscenities.

And to the crowd at some nervous rustling meeting
Grates through the speaker's teeth when trouble starts.
Pain has invaded the city and gapes at its heart.

And you, under whose hands now five years gone
In the same room in the same restless dawn
I lay, now lie under whose hands, whose thighs
And stare at the wall with the same aching eyes?

1962

The Survivor

The skull in my hands is my life's. It stares at me.
My child peers out through its eyes, my wife's lips move
Across the polished bone where its lips should be;
Her hair is soft on the crown and burns for love.

We are held in a single death: child, husband, wife,
Mixed blood, mixed feelings, fingers mixed and minds
Burn in a single flame across our lives,
And I am left with a delicate skull in my hands.

Strange that a bone should flame as though dipped in pitch,
Strangely intense in death, strange tenderness
In blood that once leapt to a cheek now cold to my touch.
Death clasps them bone to bone against his chest.

Only the skull is left, the last hard fact
That turns in my hands, in my blood, under my skin,
Pacing my life like a traveller who taps
The earth and cries, 'Dear mother, let me in'.

1960

III

The Waterfall

In the soft afternoon air my soft afternoon neighbour
Starts screaming from the belly of his throat.
Only before of cars, his daughters, liquor,
Now he is yelling his head off with a voice
Like night, like nightmare: 'No. No. No. No. No.'

No more. The soft street sways with the explosion.
The sun survives the clouds. Birds reassume
Their privileges. The traffic mumbles on
Like sleep. No tears, no explanations.
Only that voice from behind the sheet of the waterfall,
The lost thing from the cave with a mouth like a navel:
     'NO.'

Under the skein of the street its echoes flow.

1963

The Bad Dream and the Photograph

Even in sleep your shadow watches me,
Your whisper rustles through the sleeping room
As though you moved in silks. Why keep on trying?
Nothing can turn you full-face to the noon.

I fool myself with pains you cannot feel.
You are contorted on another wheel.

It is some illness haunts you. Thin as water
Your cry draws out my pain and breath in one.
The whole thing flickers to a halt. You fade
And I perhaps might gape to find you gone.

But only stir and know you will not sleep
Gazing obliquely through the chilly dawn.
For what? Your uneasy trance will never break,
Your smiling never save you from the dark,
Nor I, for knowing you, be less alone.

1956

The Vigil

The spider love that transubstantiates all
Donne

You stand in the first dumbness of the snow
As finely, the gauze drop in pantomime,
All detail fades upon your startled face
And back to darkness line and colour flow.

The final trance and rapture of the bone
Has come. What rain on stone and age in us
Raddle the snow dispenses equally –
Years towards death in one short afternoon.

The mouth lifts at one corner, on the crown
Regally twists the hair against the white
Stark imposition of a nervous fit,
Ageing in frozen tumult like a clown.

You mime stock-still your final comic pose:
Seduced by the earthy widower of spades
Slowly to dissolution and the blank
Tumbler's lust for stature and repose.

1954

A. ALVAREZ

The Catharsis

It is the tenderness you feel you know
You may have had the tenderness you miss.

Still in the mask you wear your tongue can go
Raptly to themes the audience won't guess

Creating from those fragments of thin air
Within the head's O what you might have been.

You are not less because they cannot share
All that you are and tell what they have seen.

Yet they're agog. Your eloquence will flow
Beyond the measure pacing your distress

Till it breaks down the limits of your care
And finally you relish what you seem

And are to your last sense all you forego:
Love. The particular. No more no less.

1953

39

The Fortunate Fall

Perhaps Eve in the garden knew the sun
With her whole flesh, and pruned the rose's soul –
The thing was thornless, pliable, like Eve –
And she the garden whence all flowers sprung.

But Adam knew her as the fruit he stole,
The apple, sleeping, God made him conceive.
His side and eyes were opened. They were bare,
The tree despoiled and knowledge risen whole.

Before she even fumbled with the leaves
Adam was finished. Of course, she had a flair
For fumbling that was folly to oppose,
Tricky, pleading, knowing. Why should he grieve?

So he chose for her, chose his own despair.
Her hair, like rain, closed on the thorny rose.

1953

A Cemetery in New Mexico

To Alfred Alvarez, dead, 1957

Softly the dead stir, call, through the afternoon.
The soil lies too light upon them and the wind
Blows through the earth as though the earth were pines.

My own blood in a heavy northern death
Sleeps with the rain and clay and dark, thick shrubs,
Where the spirit fights for movement as for breath.

But among these pines the crosses grow like ferns,
Frail sprouting wood and mottled, slender stones,
And the wind moves, through shadows moves the sun.

Delicate the light, the air, a breathing
Joins the mourners to the dead in one light sleep:
I watch as I would watch a blind man sleeping,

And remember the day the creaking ropes let slip
My grandfather's heavy body into his grave,
And the rain came down as we shovelled the earth on the lid.

The clods fell final and flat as a blow in the wind
While the mourners patiently hunched against the rain.
There were Hebrew prayers I didn't understand.

In Willesden Cemetery, honoured, wealthy, prone,
Unyielding and remote, he bides his time.
And carved above his head is my own name.

Over and over again the thing begins:
My son at night now frets us with his cries
When dark above his crib the same face leans.

And even here in this clear afternoon
The dead are moving like wind among the pines;
They touch my mouth, they curl along my spine.
They are waiting for me. Why won't they call my name?

1958

Dying

Adapted from the Ancient Egyptian

Death is before me today
           like recovering from an illness
           and going into the garden
Death

           the odour of myrrh
           a sail's curving shadow on a windy day
Death

           like the scent of the lotus
           like lingering on the shore of drunkenness
Death

           a quick, cool stream
           a soldier coming home
Death

           like a break in the clouds
           a bird's flight into the unknown
Death

           like homesickness
           like homecoming after captivity.

1970

ROY FULLER

To My Brother

A pistol is cocked and levelled in the room.
The running window opens to the sounds
Of hooters from the Thames at Greenwich, doom

Descends the chimney in the rustling grounds
Of soot. The Globe edition of Pope you gave me
Is open on the chair arm. There are bounds

To feeling in this suburb, but nothing can save me
Tonight from the scenic railway journey over
Europe to locate my future grave: the

Arming world rushes by me where you hover
Behind right shoulders on the German border,
Or at the *Terminus* removing a cover,

Taking perhaps your memories, like a warder,
The memories of our responsible youth,
To give the refugees a sense of order.

My real world also has a base of truth:
Soldiers with labial sores, a yellowish stone
Built round the common into cubes, uncouth

Reverberations from a breaking bone,
The fear of living in the body. Is it
Here we start or end? Tonight my own

Thoughts pay a merely temporary visit
To the state where objects have lost their power of motion,
Their laws which terrify and can elicit

A furious tale from casual emotion,
Where life with instruments surveys the maps
Of cut-out continent and plasticine ocean,

Far from the imminent and loud collapse
Of culture, prophesied by liberals,
Whose guilty ghosts can never say perhaps.

This kind of world Pope, with his quartz and shells,
Constructed in his azure Twickenham grotto,
Which in the daytime entertained the belles,

But glowed and writhed to form a personal motto
At night, with brute distraction in its lair;
The mirrors flattering as part of the plot: 'O

Alex, you are handsome; you have power
First to arrange a world and then to abstract
Its final communication; virtues shower

From the exercise of your genius; the pact
Of friendship is good and all your enemies only
In opposition to civilization act.'

When I am falsely elevated and lonely,
And the effort of making contact even with you
Is helped by distance, the life is finely

Shown which holds on contract, and the true
Perish in cities which revolve behind
Like dust.
             The window explodes, and now
The centre land mass breathes a tragic wind.

War Poet

Swift had pains in his head.
Johnson dying in bed
Tapped the dropsy himself.
Blake saw a flea and an elf.
Tennyson could hear the shriek
Of a bat. Pope was a freak.
Emily Dickinson stayed
Indoors for a decade.
Water inflated the belly
Of Hart Crane, and of Shelley.
Coleridge was a dope.
Southwell died on a rope.
Byron had a round white foot.
Smart and Cowper were put
Away. Lawrence was a fidget.
Keats was almost a midget.
Donne, alive in his shroud,
Shakespeare, in the coil of a cloud,
Saw death very well as he
Came crab-wise, dark and massy.
I envy not only their talents
And fertile lack of balance
But the appearance of choice
In their sad and fatal voice.

To My Wife

The loud mechanical voices of the sirens
Lure me from sleep and on the heath, like stars,
Moths fall into a mounting shaft of light.
Aircraft whirr over and then the night stays quiet;
The moon is peeled of cloud, its gold is changed
On stone for silver and the cap of sky
Glitters like quartz, impersonal and remote.
This surface is the same: the clock's bland face,
Its smiling moustaches, hide the spring, knotted
Like muscles, and the crouching jungle hammer.

The same but so different with you not here.
This evening when I turned from the clothes you left,
Empty and silk, the souls of swallows flickered
Against the glass of our house: I felt no better
Along the tree-massed alleys where I saw
The long pale legs on benches in the dark.
It was no vague nostalgia which I breathed
Between the purple colloids of the air:
My lust was as precise and fierce as that of
The wedge-headed jaguar or the travelling Flaubert.

But I only encountered the ghosts of the suburb,
Those ghosts you know and who are real and walk
And talk in the small public gardens, by the tawdry
Local monuments; the Witch and Big Head
And the others, fleeting and familiar as
Our memories and ambitions, and just as dead.
Being alone they stopped me; Big Head first.
Removing her unbelievable hat, she showed me
What before I had only conjectured, and she whispered:
O lucky you – you might have been born like this.

I knew it was true, but, hurrying on, the Witch
Lifted her cane and barred the way: she is
Lean and very dirty but hanging round
That skeleton are rags of flesh still handsome.
Moving her lips madly and in a foreign tone she said:
Oh do not hope, boy – you will come to this.
I ran, being certain that she had not erred,
Back to our room where now the only noise
Is the icy modulated voice of Mozart
And the false clock ticking on the mantelpiece.

Now in the bubble of London whose glass will soon
Smear into death, at the still-calm hour of four,
I see the shadows of our life, the Fates
We narrowly missed, our possible destiny.
I try to say that love is more solid than
Our bodies, but I only want you here.
*I know they created love and that the rest
Is ghosts; war murders love* – I really say.
But dare I write it to you who have said it
Always and have no consolation from the ghosts?

Saturday Night in a Sailors' Home

A honeycomb of cabins, boxes, cells,
To which each man retires alone.
A snatch of singing, like a groan,
Broken off quickly. Sour, damp smells.

The cell is never dark. There are
The drummings of fluid on enamel.
Behind the separating panel
The anxious voices speak in prayer:

I wish I could be sick and *Please
Shake me at five: God, what an hour
To wake!* The drugs have lost their power:
Still crawling in the naked light
Are the obscene realities.
The coughing goes on all the night.

The Middle of a War

My photograph already looks historic.
The promising youthful face, the matelot's collar,
Say 'This one is remembered for a lyric.
His place and period – nothing could be duller.'

Its position is already indicated –
The son or brother in the album; pained
The expression and the garments dated,
His fate so obviously preordained.

The original turns away: as horrible thoughts,
Loud fluttering aircraft slope above his head
At dusk. The ridiculous empires break like biscuits.
Ah, life has been abandoned by the boats –
Only the trodden island and the dead
Remain, and the once inestimable caskets.

Harbour Ferry

The oldest and simplest thoughts
Rise with the antique moon:
How she enamels men
And artillery under her sphere,
Eyelids and hair and throats
Rigid in love and war;
How this has happened before.

And how the lonely man
Raises his head and shudders
With a brilliant sense of the madness,
The age and shape of his planet,
Wherever his human hand,
Whatever his set of tenets,
The long and crucial minute.

Tonight the moon has risen
Over a quiet harbour,
Through twisted iron and labour,
Lighting the half-drowned ships.
Oh surely the fatal chasm
Is closer, the furious steps
Swifter? The silver drips

From the angle of the wake:
The moon is flooding the faces.
The moment is over: the forces
Controlling lion nature
Look out of the eyes and speak:
Can you believe in a future
Left only to rock and creature?

The Green Hills of Africa

The green, humped, wrinkled hills: with such a look
Of age (or youth) as to erect the hair.
They crouch above the ports or on the plain,
Beneath the matchless skies; are like a strange
Girl's shoulders suddenly against your hands.
What covers them so softly, vividly?
They break at the sea in a cliff, a mouth of red:
Upon the plain are unapproachable,
Furrowed and huge, dramatically lit.

And yet one cannot be surprised at what
The hills contain. The girls run up the slope,
Their oiled and shaven heads like caramels.
Behind, the village, with its corrugated
Iron, the wicked habit of the store.
The villagers cough, the sacking blows from the naked
Skin of a child, a white scum on his lips.
The youths come down in feathers from the peak.
And over all a massive frescoed sky.

The poisoner proceeds by tiny doses,
The victim weaker and weaker but uncomplaining.
Soon they will only dance for money, will
Discover more and more things can be sold.
What gods did you expect to find here, with
What healing powers? What subtle ways of life?
No, there is nothing but the forms and colours,
And the emotion brought from a world already
Dying of what starts to infect the hills.

The Photographs

The faces in the obscene photographs
Gaze out with no expression: they are like
The dead, who always look as though surprised
In a most intimate attitude. The man
And woman in the photograph have faces
Of corpses; their positions are of love –
Which we have taken. I remember how
Once, coming from the waves, I found you chill
Beneath the *maillot* in a sun-warmed house;
And on such memories are now imposed
The phantasies engendered by these two.

Evening: the rows of anxious aircraft wait,
Speckled with tiny brown and crimson birds;
The plain extends to an escarpment lit
Softly as by a steady candle flame;
And then there is the great curve of the earth
And, after, you, whom two seas and a war
Divides.
      The dust blows up. As long as those
Photographs poison my imagination
I shall not dare to catch my countenance
In any mirror; for it seems to me
Our faces, bodies – both of us – are dead.

The White Conscript and the Black Conscript

I do not understand
Your language, nor you mine.
If we communicate
It is hardly the word that matters or the sign,
But what I can divine.

Are they in London white
Or black? How do you know,
Not speaking my tongue, the names
Of our tribes? It could be as easily a blow
As a match you give me now.

Under this moon which the curdled
Clouds permit often to shine
I can see more than your round cap,
Your tallness, great eyes and your aquiline
Nose, and the skin, light, fine.

The British must be wicked:
They fight. I have been brought
From our wide pastures, from
The formal rules of conduct I was taught;
Like a beast I have been caught.

If only I could tell you
That in my country there
Are millions as poor as you
And almost as unfree: if I could share
Our burdens of despair!

For I who seem so rich,
So free, so happy, am
Like you the most despised.
And I would not have had you come
As I most loath have come.

Among our tribe, like yours,
There are some bad, some good –
That is all I am able to say:
Because you would not believe me if I could
Tell you it is for you, the oppressed, the good
Only desire to die.

What is Terrible

Life at last I know is terrible:
The innocent scene, the innocent walls and light
And hills for me are like the cavities
Of surgery or dreams. The visible might
Vanish, for all it reassures, in white.

This apprehension has come slowly to me,
Like symptoms and bulletins of sickness. I
Must first be moved across two oceans, then
Bored, systematically and sickeningly,
In a place where war is news. And constantly

I must be threatened with what is certainly worse:
Peril and death, but no less boring. And
What else? Besides my fear, my misspent time,
My love, hurt and postponed, there is the hand
Moving the empty glove; the bland

Aspect of nothing disguised as something; that
Part of living incommunicable,
For which we try to find vague adequate
Images, and which, after all,
Is quite surprisingly communicable.

Because in the clear hard light of war the ghosts
Are seen to be suspended by wires, and in
The old house the attic is empty: and the furious
Inner existence of objects and even
Ourselves is largely a myth: and for the sin

To blame our fathers, to attribute vengeance
To the pursuing chorus, and to live
In a good and tenuous world of private values,
Is simply to lie when only truth can give
Continuation in time to bread and love.

For what is terrible is the obvious
Organization of life: the oiled black gun,
And what it cost; the destruction of Europe by
Its councils; the unending justification
Of that which cannot be justified, what is done.

The year, the month, the day, the minute, at war
Is terrible and my participation
And that of all the world is terrible.
My living now must bear the laceration
Of the herd, and always will. What's done

To me is done to many. I can see
No ghosts, but only the fearful actual
Lives of my comrades. If the empty whitish
Horror is ever to be flushed and real,
It must be for them and changed by them all.

The Statue

The noises of the harbour die, the smoke is petrified
Against the thick but vacant, fading light, and shadows slide
From under stone and iron, darkest now. The last birds glide.

Upon this black-boned, white-splashed, far receding vista of
   grey
Is an equestrian statue, by the ocean, trampling the day,
Its green bronze flaked like petals, catching night before the
   bay.

Distilled from some sad, endless, sordid period of time,
As from the language of disease might come a consummate
   rhyme,
It tries to impose its values on the port and on the lime –

The droppings that by chance and from an uncontrollable
And savage life have formed a patina upon the skull;
Abandoned, have blurred a bodied vision once thought spare
   but full –

On me, as authority recites to boys the names of queens.
Shall I be dazzled by the dynasties, the gules and greens,
The unbelievable art, and not recall their piteous means?

Last night I sailed upon that sea whose starting place is here,
Evaded the contraptions of the enemy, the mere
Dangers of water, saw the statue and the plinth appear.

Last night between the crowded, stifling decks I watched a
   man,
Smoking a big curved pipe, who contemplated his great wan
And dirty feet while minute after tedious minute ran –

This in the city now, whose floor is permanent and still,
Among the news of history and sense of an obscure will,
Is all the image I can summon up, my thought's rank kill;

As though there dominated this sea's threshold and this night
Not the raised hooves, the thick snake neck, the profile, and
   the might,
The wrought, eternal bronze, the dead protagonist, the fight,

But that unmoving, pale but living shape that drops no tears,
Ridiculous and haunting, which each epoch reappears,
And is what history is not. O love, O human fears!

During a Bombardment by V-Weapons

The little noises of the house:
Drippings between the slates and ceiling;
From the electric fire's cooling,
Tickings; the dry feet of a mouse:

These at the ending of a war
Have power to alarm me more
Than the ridiculous detonations
Outside the gently coughing curtains.

And, love, I see your pallor bears
A far more pointed threat than steel.
Now all the permanent and real
Furies are settling in upstairs.

The Civilization

By their frock-coated leaders,
By the frequency of their wars,
By the depth of their hunger,
Their numberless refugees,
And the brevity of their verse,
They were distinguished.

Their revolutions
Were thwarted by kisses.
The cold mathematicians
Aged into blurred philosophers.
Their poets choked on
The parallel of past calamities.

Their funeral customs, art,
Physique, and secret
Societies, unequal:
Their doom inevitable.
Ambiguous as dreams
Their symbolic poetry.

Yes, it had happened
Before. Ill-pictured leaders,
Food-queues in foodless places,
Migration to areas
Of moderate terror,
Monotonous poems.

Then horses galloping
Over burned foundations,
Ascetic communities,

The improbable moon,
Death from a cut,
Bleak, eroded spaces;

And eventually the strangers,
With the luxury of spices,
Effective weapons,
Their tales of travel,
Their ikons of leaders,
Their epic verse.

Nursery Rhyme

Than the outlook of the ulcer
Nothing could be falser,
And the way of living of
The psychosis is not love.

In the good society
Morbid art's not necessary.
It's a sick subhuman voice
Comes from Kafka, Proust and Joyce.

After much analysis
Freud found he could not tell lies.
But in most there is no truth
After the initial tooth.

Though among both poor and rich
Are found the bully and the bitch,
Only those who haven't got
Can be free of what they've not.

Round the massive legs of man
Scuttle all the little men,
Busy planning for what's great
Their own ludicrous charred fate.

Hymn

Tell us how we can arrive at
Secrets locked behind the veil –
Byron's foot and James's privates,
Why Pope was pale.

Why we cannot still recall
What we did in bed with father –
Or what nurse said through the wall,
If you'd rather.

Put us in the way of knowing
Why we work our hair to toupees,
While the idle rich are flowing
In drop-head coupés.

Tell us why we wish for peace
While our nation swells its forces,
Why in others lust to crease
Us madly courses.

Now from all the ghastly land
Rise the swirling tea-leaves of
Rooks, and syphilitic stand
Stone boys of love.

Over bile-hued fields of May
Shines the day-time moon, a bone,
From them in this sad today
A light has flown.

While the leaders point, enraged,
And their people groan like ice,
Quietly sit the mad, engaged
With phantom lice.

Teach us thus to live in patience,
If you cannot teach us more,
Till progressive cerebration
Stops with war.

Translation

Now that the barbarians have got as far as Picra,
And all the new music is written in the twelve-tone scale,
And I am anyway approaching my fortieth birthday,
    I will dissemble no longer.

I will stop expressing my belief in the rosy
Future of man, and accept the evidence
Of a couple of wretched wars and innumerable
    Abortive revolutions.

I will cease to blame the stupidity of the slaves
Upon their masters and nurture, and will say,
Plainly, that they are enemies to culture,
    Advancement and cleanliness.

From progressive organizations, from quarterlies
Devoted to daring verse, from membership of
Committees, from letters of various protest
    I shall withdraw forthwith.

When they call me reactionary I shall smile,
Secure in another dimension. When they say
'Cinna has ceased to matter' I shall know
    How well I reflect the times.

The ruling class will think I am on their side
And make friendly overtures, but I shall retire
To the side farther from Picra and write some poems
    About the doom of the whole boiling.

Anyone happy in this age and place
Is daft or corrupt. Better to abdicate
From a material and spiritual terrain
    Fit only for barbarians.

Inaction

Writers entrapped by teatime fame and by commuters' comforts.
Marianne Moore

A strange dog trots into the drive, sniffs, turns
And pees against a mudguard of my car.
I see this through the window, past *The Times*,
And drop my toast and impotently glare.

But indignation gives way to unease.
Clearly the dog, not merely impudent,
Was critical of man's activities,
Mine in particular, I'm forced to grant.

And so the entertainment of the morning
Headlines is temporarily spoiled for me:
During my coffee I must heed their warning,
The fate of millions take half seriously.

Inadequate, I know, this old concern,
Only productive of a quickened pulse,
A hanging jacket that gives one a turn.
The sneering dog demanded something else.

A Wet Sunday in Spring

Symptoms at high altitudes:
Emaciation and overstrain.
Life at high latitudes: small wingless flies
Capable of living for long periods
In a frozen state.

I sit in the inventive temperate zone,
Raised only by the city's floors of culture,
Watching the rain bombard the lilac, feeling
The radio come in round me like a tide.
Deafness let Beethoven escape the tyranny
Of concord: some such mutation should exclude this age
From having to admit the possibility
Of happiness.
              The ivory-horned chestnut
Effortlessly assumes its tasks; the rain
Is perpendicular and horribly fertile;
The embattled green proliferates like cells.
I think feebly of man's wrong organizations,
Incurable leaders, nature lying in wait
For weakness like an animal or germ,
And aircraft growling in the summer air.

Florestan to Leonora

Our shadows fall beyond the empty cage.
The Minister has gone and I am left
To try to live with your heroic age.

I spare a thought, my dear, for you who must
Go home to change the jackboots for a skirt
And put the pistol on its nail to rust;

But mainly think of my impossible task.
My own love might have tried what yours achieved:
It cannot bear the gift it did not ask.

After the trumpet I felt, in our embrace,
I had been cheated of the captured's right
To innocent inaction and to face

A suffering unjust as a sarcoma.
Did you never conceive that it was possible
To like incarceration? In this trauma

Of the imprisoning era there must be
Some prisoners – for torturers to visit,
To wear the pallor and the beards of free

Philosophers, and tap on streaming walls
Their selfless ineffective messages
Concerning liberty to brutish cells.

When the mob sang of brotherhood and joy
I was embarrassed, more so when I saw
The near-erotic answer in your eye.

You take my hand as though I ought to live;
And lead me out to that alarming world
Which, the oppressor dead, the sensitive

Can find inimical no longer. Yes,
Our values must shrivel to the size of those
Held by a class content with happiness;

And warmed by our children, full of bread and wine,
I shall dream of the discipline of insomnia
And an art of symbols, starved and saturnine.

One and Many

Awake at five, I am surprised to see
Across the flocculent and winter dark
Windows already yellow; and am touched
By the unconscious solidarity
Of the industrious world of normal men
With art's insomnia and spleen,
As unaccountably as when
A long-dead negro plays through a machine.

I think of galleries lined with Renaissance man's
Discovery of physique, and jealously wonder
Why now it is impossible to show
Human existence in its natural stance –
The range of burgher, tart and emperor,
Set among withers, game, brocade,
Merely as themselves, not emblems for
A stringent world the artist never made.

Did the imagination then proceed
Quite naturally with a cast of men
Resembling the creator, who played out
Not anguish at the prospect of a deed
Ending a loathed society, nor that
Consideration shown by fear,
But were ambitious, usual, fat,
Pugnacious, comic, worldly, cavalier?

Not really so: the eye of art was cocked
Always from low and lonely vantages,
And the great boots and thighs, the glittering chests,
Taken for granted by their owners, blocked

A sky full of desired irrelevant stars
Whose enigmatic message lay
In wait until the rogues and czars
Fell ranting in a dynasty's decay.

And now art's only living figure broods
On the ensanguined falling moon until
The opposite horizon cracks and lights
Go out: over sapped and far-transported foods
I read of crises and prepare for living
In that strict hierarchy of
A miser body made for giving
And which prepares for war desiring love.

Monologue in Autumn

With yellow teeth the hunter tears and crunches
Whole boughs of the quince, then walks away,
His hind legs on a mannequin's straight line.
The clipped back (ample as a bed, unyielding
Save for a slight threat like an anchored ship)
Returns what always astonishes – the warmth
Of a new embrace.

         And you arrive. I help
To raise your body in its carapace
Of steel and leather. Then I see you move,
A centaur, down the slopes towards the plain
Where in the mist the sun already hangs
Its monstrous copper and autumnal shape.

You fade. I turn across the leaf-crumbed lawn:
Under the mulberry the gales have torn
A cat gnaws the purple lining of the pelt
It emptied yesterday.

         And now the house:
First the twin balustrades and then the busts
Whose formal curls and noses are as rough
As if their existence truly were marine
Under the window's random lights. Inside
The books propound what all books must propound:
Whether man shall accept the authority of God
Or of his senses.

         In the drawing room
The fire sadly burns for no one: soon
Your guests will descend, taste tea on Sunday tongues;
Their lives and mine and yours go on with talk,
The disposition of chairs and lamps, the opened
Doors to the terrace, the order of good-nights.

Hard to imagine that the ambassador,
Your cousin, lives at this same hour among
Furs, fuming breaths, ardours of moral striving;
That such half world exists for which our own
Has manufactured all its cruel swords and faces
Whose profits surround us here as love affairs,
Portable sketching outfits, hair arranged
Like savages and scented with the whole
Resources of science.

                Yet this must account
For what I feel, in love with you, within
This house and season – that residual sadness
After bare rooms and trees have been subtracted
And love has learned the trick of suffering
Its object's relative indifference.
Why, as you always ask, should I so dread
What threatens from the rivalry of two
Crude ways of life, two grotesque empires, whose
Ideals, diplomacy and soldiery
We must despise? But merely to formulate
The question seems to me to answer it,
And show that shameful collective death as quite
Other than what we think of in the dawn –
The torturer that will test us in our cell.

I open the piano, sound a note,
Remember dreams. How could you come to grow
In my imagination (that must have been
My wish) so sallow and in such a place –
As strange and circumstantial as the future?
You said the words too wild to be recalled,
Lay back and gently died.

                You will return,
Your horse not sweating quite enough to mark

The lapse of time. I shall forbear to ask
The question that makes pain a certainty,
But merely look with the avoiding eyes
Of a Cesario or Cordelia.

And dinner will stretch into drowsiness,
Owls swing like theatre fairies past the moon
Whose battered lantern lights the tops of woods
And shines along the calm, dividing sea,
Painting with fire the armour in the harbours
Which lie encircled by their snowy lands
And multiplicity of helpless wills.

The uninvited images invade
The separate and sleeping heads: dead branches
Threading the sockets of those equine skulls
Whose riders perished in the useless war,
Whose teeth are rattled in their open jaws
By tempests from sastrugi, and whose foals
Stream through what whitens their brazil-nut eyes
Towards savannahs where the planet holds
Only inhuman species to its pap.

On the Mountain

I

Why red, why red? I ask myself, observing
A girl's enamelled nails, not understanding
The convention – an unrealistic art.

I live in a suburb of the capital,
A hill of villas, and sometimes note such things;
Old enough to remember better days.

The stoics have virtually disappeared.
I like to think myself the last of them,
Shaken but not devoured by ghastly omens.

The theatres are given up to leg shows
And gladiatorial games. The savage beasts
Are weary with the number of their victims.

In poetry the last trace of conviction
Has long since been extinguished. Round the temples
Are crowds of flautists, eunuchs and raving females.

The decoration of the baths and other
Edifices of importance is assigned
To those same careless slaves who mix the mortar.

The so-called educated classes share
The superstitions and amusements of
The vulgar, gawping at guts and moaning singers.

Atrocious taxes to 'defend' the frontiers;
Fixing maximum prices yet deploring the black market
– These the preoccupations of the state.

And the alarming aspect of imperial
Succession! The imperial madness! O
My country, how long shall we bear such things?

I find a little comfort in recalling
That complaints of evil times are found in every
Age which has left a literature behind:

And the lyric is always capable
Of rejuvenation (as is the human heart),
Even in times of general wretchedness.

II

In my garden, at the risk of annoying my cat,
I rescue a fledgling: as it squeaks, I see
That its tongue is like something inside a watch.

They would not find it odd, those Others –
Mysterious community, not outside
And not within the borders of the empire;

Not the barbarians precisely nor
The slaves: indeed, from their strange treason no
Mind is exempt . . . even the emperor's!

Could I believe? Surrender to the future,
The inevitability of the future – which
Nevertheless can only come by martyrdom?

Respect those priestly leaders, arguing
Whether the Second Person of the Three
Is equal or subordinate to the First?

While in their guarded monasteries they lift
Their greasy cassocks to ecstatic girls –
Under the bed their secret box of coin.

I suppose their creed must conquer in the end
Because it gives the simplest and most complete
Answer to all men ask in these bad years.

Is there a life beyond this life? Must art
Be the maidservant of morality?
And will the humble triumph? Yes. Yes. Yes.

Disgusting questions, horrible reply;
Deplorable the course of history:
And yet we cannot but regard with awe

The struggle of the locked and rival systems,
Involving the entire geography
Of the known world, through epochs staggeringly
    prolonged.

To name our cities after poets, or
To hasten the destruction of the species –
The debate continues chronic and unresolved.

III

How rapidly one's thoughts get out of hand!
With my unsatisfactory physique
I watch the blossom through the blinding rain,

Cringe the while at the shoddy workmanship
Of the piddling gutter – typical of the times –
And stroke with skeleton hand the mortal fur.

It is as hard to realize where we are
As for the climber on the famous peak
For whom the familiar outline is no more

The record of a deadly illness or
The tearing organs of a bird of prey
But merely boredom, breathing, prudence, stones.

Note: this poem is greatly indebted to Moses Hadas's translation of
Burckhardt's *The Age of Constantine the Great*.

Versions of Love

'My love for you has faded' – thus the Bad
Quarto, the earliest text, whose midget page
Derived from the imperfect memories
Of red-nosed, small-part actors
Or the atrocious shorthand of the age.

However, the far superior Folio had
'My love for you was fated' – thus implying
Illicit passion, a tragic final act.
And this was printed from the poet's own
Foul papers, it was reckoned;
Supported by the reading of the Second
Quarto, which had those sombre words exact.

Such evidence was shaken when collation
Showed that the Folio copied slavishly
The literals of that supposedly
Independent Quarto. Thus one had to go
Back to the first text of all.

'My love for you has faded' – quite impossible.
Scholars produced at last the emendation:
'My love for you fast endured.'
Our author's ancient hand that must have been
Ambiguous and intellectual
Foxed the compositors of a certainty.
And so the critical editions gave
Love the sound status that she ought to have
In poetry so revered.

But this conjecture cannot quite destroy
The question of what the poet really wrote
In the glum middle reaches of his life:
Too sage, too bald, too fearful of fiasco
To hope beyond his wife,
Yet aching almost as promptly as a boy.

At T. S. Eliot's Memorial Service

A man comes on the stage clad in a robe different from all others, with lute in hand on which he plays, and thus chants the Great Mysteries, not knowing what he says.
Jessie L. Weston: *From Ritual to Romance*

Arches cut across each other,
    open out within each other, till
Winter sky the shade of old men's
    hair appears beyond the final sill.

Rectangles of iron-tubing
    for the pensile lamps draw down the eye
To the choir-stalls' vandyke timber
    and their submarine upholstery.

Here the lights themselves seem gloomy:
    golden stalks with single crimson flowers.
Distant pallid busts the monu-
    ments of poets longer dead than ours.

In the drama set to show the
    spirit's primacy and endlessness
Piping choir-boys pustular re-
    mind one of its transitory dress.

Revolutionary writer
    of my youth, how far must it have been
From imagination so to
    see you to the brink of the unseen;

And in your relating of the
    myth to find at last that it was thus
Fell the strange and frightening ad-
    venture in the Castle Perilous –

Which is fraught, we're made to under-
    stand, with danger indefinable:
Details vary; sometimes on the
    altar there is laid a lifeless shell . . .

Suddenly I notice that the
    arms that isolate me in my place
Are the backward-spreading wings of
    angels each with polished plump-cheeked face.

Simple craftsman's image, words and
    chords by more sophisticated pens,
Celebrate the sad illusion
    that the mortal nerves and brain make sense.

Tributory bowler on its
    not entirely unaccustomed head,
Leaving through the great West Door, bells
    muffled for the now-accepted dead,

All is changed until I see that
    it's Victoria Street and not the Square
Lies before me, purgatory-
    crowded, hideous in the sharpening air –

Half expecting one to hail me,
    marks of mould upon him, grave of tone:
'Wounded still the Ruler, water-
    less the land, omnipotent the bone.'

Apple Tree

I puzzle why the flowering tree
Is also in song, until I see
Each flower's stigma is a bee.

Great magnet, drawing from the lawn
The scattered sparrows when I yawn,
I wonder whence your force is drawn –

And then observe the vertical
That sinks into the emerald ball,
Down which the birds would doubtless fall

Were it not full of lymph, transpiring
Through the boughs' dense, right-angled wiring
In scent and incandescent firing.

Pulling the curtains when I wake
I watch snow tumbling, flake on flake,
From the sky's azure, unisled lake.

It drifts among the buoys of red
At anchor in the tulip bed,
And on the limbs from which it's shed –

Limbs hugely knuckled, crooked, lined,
What ecstasy for you to find
The fair skin brush your old dark rind.

Logic of Dreams

Waking to the scarcely lit curtain, the plop
Of a letter, the worn familiar mask,
It is hard to imagine how dreams contrive
To deposit one nude before mad girl-faced apes.

Five minutes after waking I remember it
And, hung over the bowl, am lost in strangeness.
A moment later it has gone beyond recall
In my head reflected in the dusky mirror.

How much more convincing, the time of dreams.
Here are my mother and my son's child together;
Here I am still shattered by jealousy
In a passion that only time has changed.

I realized I loved my long-vanished friend
And showed him clumsily the vanished love,
Feeling a warm bulk in his dead shoulders
That for me they never had in life.

Once more, since miraculously she was still alive,
I had to wish my suffering mother dead.

The age's disaster we had always escaped
At last engulfed us and ghastly it was.
Yet because we lived still in the burning and torture
We knew it in our hearts to be simply a dream.

So often she told me she was chased by lions;
We smiled at the involuntary symbolism.
But to be with her, failing to save her from lions,
That is a terrible fate and meaning.

I was sure it was not her getting in the window,
Because I heard her moving about in the kitchen.

Turning into the corridor and finding
In the embrasure a waiting, silent figure,
And fleeing . . . the influence of art:
But an art rooted insanely in life, not dreams.

Astonishing that my cries should wake her,
Since they were powerless in the dream.

Impoverished wakening to unrecalled dreams:
Start of a day empty of dreaming's source.

Astapovo, 1910

The old man who died at the railway
Station, ready to leave for somewhere
Else, said: 'Whoever is happy is
Right.' The birch groves silvered the land to
Asia, and the peasants were about
To throw in their lot with factory
Hands and the cheesed-off military.

But at the moment he was fleeing
A marital sexuality
Turned grotesque with age. Locomotives
With top-hats for funnels, that had run
Down Anna Karenina, passed to
And fro while he lay dying, dreaming
Of the end of all authority.

His diary was found to observe:
'Only old people and children, free
From sexual lusts, live a true life.'
No doubt he was off to find it. The
Rest of humanity, he believed,
Was merely a factory for the
Continuation of animals.

Utopian textile mills, cigar
Smoking women, students with grenades
Tagged 'Czar', apostles of deep breathing,
Vegetarianism – all these
Had to flourish and then be subsumed
In the amendment of bankers' aims
And an electrical policy.

'Many people think that poetry
May be found only in sexual
Life. All true poetry is always
Outside it.' One sees what he meant, though
Reluctantly disagreeing. Make
Poetry out of this, said the head
Of heavy industry, with reason.

Each generation is unhappy
In its own way; looks on its children
With complacent envy. 'For you we
Expropriated the unjust and
Rich. Why aren't you laughing?' But the young
Feel no more than poets and old men
That matters accord with their vision.

Ambiguities of Travel

And will you really wake at the hotel
With the mountain in the garden and the crippled
Gardener? And go to see the wall-paintings
Of the wall-eyed flautists, and the pink sandstone
Water nymph with vulva-exposing embroideries,
And the silk banner (reconstruction) of Lord Kanishka?

Poetry is something between the dream
And its interpretation. Through pleached boughs
Of blossoming, still vivid your pantisocratic
Imaginings, how hurtful to think
Of the past dragging its foot to meet you,
As though a mirror stood at the pathway's end.

A saying of Kanishka: 'Human love –
So much beauty lavished on so much goodness.'
Dear child, it's only that the colours have flaked
That the musicians are so repulsive;
And the sepulchre of the ruler was long ago
Shat on by pillaging baboons.

What song will your mind rehearse as, shaving,
You see the girl still slumbering in the striped light?
That late sonata movement where, trilling each note,
The performer's hands move farther and farther apart?
Strange, both expounding life in likenesses,
Voyaging through the other's boiling wake.

Those of Pure Origin

Ein Räthsel ist Reinentsprungenes. Auch
Der Gesang kaum darf es enthüllen. Denn
Wie du anfiengst, wirst du bleiben. – Hölderlin

A mystery are those of pure origin.
Even song may hardly unveil it.
For as you began, so you will remain. – trans. Michael Hamburger

After a throbbing night, the house still dark, pull
Back the curtains, see the cherry standing there –
Grain of the paper under wash of rain-clouds.

No, our disguises are not intended to
Deceive. On the contrary. And could you name
Us we shouldn't be compelled to appear so
Confusingly – smothered in white stars, whistling
Hymn tunes, putting out scaly paws to attract
Attention. Under comic aliases –
Even the specific for insomnia:
Peppermint, lime blossom, betony, scullcap –
We entice you into our dissident realms.
The staggering plots you invent in hours
Abbreviated by anxiety are
Hatched by our logic. Just as when you try to
Talk with the girl of fifteen we tilt her shoe
Inward to imply her different order.

For it's *your* world we're expounding. Don't mistake
Our endeavours. We can't tell you where you're from.
Indeed, despite our immanence we're the last
Who could reveal more than is there already.

Let alone where you're going! Darwin's infant
Inquired about his friend's father: 'Where does
He do his barnacles?' – assumption of a
Universal preoccupation no more
Naïve than yours, whether of indifference or
Concern. It's quite plausible that the concept
Of outside disappears outside – in that place
Where nebulae no longer have to awake
And pretend to be happy.
                              Our advice is:
Prefer the less likely explanation.
Different evenings, the evening star appearing
In different corners of the pane – conceive
No senseless revolution in the heavens
But a lucky change of erotic fortune;
A goddess steeped not in urine but in love.
And then so often you've been wrong why shouldn't
You be wrong about the extinction of man?

It's true we tend to avoid you, fatal as
You are in general to our fragility.
But sometimes one of us, whom you knew in flight
And particularly admired for his looks,
Lies down and allows the wind to blow the wrong way
His once glossy pinions. Look into his eye.
It regards you still, though fixed as well on worlds
More real than at that moment you can bear.
Of course, you'll soon take your spade and among
Pebbles, lapis worms, inter the eye from sight.

'Considering my present condition,
I can neither concentrate on poetry
Nor enjoy poetry.' That final letter
May seem a defeat after a lifetime of

94

Assuming the reality of the art.
Not to us, though it's we are the defeated.
For we boast of our patience – coral *croissants*
Anchored at last to just too heavy hill-tops;
Laboratories of finches; Galapagos
Of revelation awaiting an observer.
And you, even in the children's puzzle, are
You certain you've seen all the hidden objects?
Yes, there's the extrusion of the wall in
A clawed hump, and a grey frayed rope-end blown round
And round a bough. But what are the abstract shapes
As enigmatic in significance as
Those painters find incised from oceans by arcs
Of a parasol or enclosed from a beach
By the severe bay of a young throat and jaw?

That countenance whose eyes are as pale as if
The flesh had been clipped out to show the ash sky
Behind it. . . . The voice that unavailingly
Says: 'Do you remember taking your laundry
To the woman with elephant legs?' . . . The past
As ambiguous as hailstones in the gales
Of Spring: the future certain – the instant when
You stop being convinced of our existence,
And meaningless that blackbirds masquerade as owls,
That also in the dusk, making free of it
For assignations, jealousies (those affairs
Of energy and waiting unwearying,
Of obsession with menstrual blood), occur
The strange pre-marital flights of humans.

What does it matter that the baptistery proves
As dusty and void as bad nuts when its doors
Provide a progression of style, the basher

Of bronze breaking out from pious platitudes
Into arcades of applied geometry,
Thronged with our perfect but realistic forms?

The mad poet called us, untranslatably:
'Those of pure origin' – left you to divine
Whether we rise from phenomena or,
Perhaps more likely, also require your presence,
As the cathedral the plague, pity the war.
But how can we pretend our hemisphere-wide
Lament, the random trickling and joining of tears
On acres of glass, is entirely for your
Predicament – as your lives, borne upon the
More and more dubiously physical, move
To regions of abnegation and concern
Whose angels we are; though, under cruel casques,
Our curls, our thick, parted lips ever youthful,
Complexions marked with still unmalignant moles
Of the actual, scabs on unfolding leaves?

Diary Entries

'I'll burn it off now if you like,' said my G.P.,
Apropos of the papilloma on my thigh,
Bothersome of late. Would that all worries
Disappeared in a whiff of over-done pork!

*

A negative report on the specimen
Of urine. So am I after all to live
Into the epoch of apocalyptic beasts
And utterly depersonalized demise?

*

A good thing on waking to drink cold water
Through the nose (I read in some Yogi handbook).
A good thing also to stop writing verses
About one's ailments and daydreams of romance.

*

Dear life, I struggle awake to greet you again –
Fetching the honied hot milk, finding my father's
Cigarette-case among the debris of yesterday's pockets,
Realizing that after all it's not you that frightens us.

Homage to Balthus

What a relief to admit, as Balthus
    with his paintings, that one's poems
are utter failures, without exception.
    Even to have got down, somewhere
along your life, the continuous line
    a girl's hair makes with her arm or
the revealed white band between naked thighs
    – quite pointless in the context of
possibilities. And the small figure
    walking away on the far green
cliff while we ourselves, trivial giants
    in the foreground, watch the artist;
and to light the outflung nude the curtain
    snatched back by a big-headed dwarf;
and in a tinted street the blanched plasterer . . .
    Noble artist, it cannot be
the absence of strange intimations
    in great reality that you
lament but the eternal refusal
    of pigment, canvas, brush, to make
a world parallel to blind creation
    and replace that with its order.

ANTHONY THWAITE

Mr Cooper

Two nights in Manchester: nothing much to do,
One of them I spent partly in a pub,
Alone, quiet, listening to people who
Didn't know me. *So I told the bloody sub-*
Manager what he could do with it. . . . Mr Payne
Covers this district – you'll have met before?
Caught short, I looked for the necessary door
And moved towards it; could hear, outside, the rain.

The usual place, with every surface smooth
To stop, I suppose, the aspirations of
The man with pencil stub and dreams of YOUTH
AGED 17. And then I saw, above
The stall, a card, a local jeweller's card
Engraved with name, JEWELLER AND WATCHMENDER
FOR FIFTY YEARS, address, telephone number.
I heard the thin rain falling in the yard.

The card was on a sort of shelf, just close
Enough to let me read this on the front.
Not, I'd have said, the sort of words to engross
Even the keenest reader, nothing to affront
The public decency of Manchester.
And yet I turned it over. On the back
Were just three words in rather smudgy black
Soft pencil: MR COOPER – DEAD. The year

Grew weakly green outside, in blackened trees,
Wet grass by statues. It was ten to ten
In March in Manchester. Now, ill at ease
And made unsure of sense and judgement when

Three words could throw me, I walked back into
The bar, where nothing much had happened since
I'd left. A man was trying to convince
Another man that somehow someone knew

Something that someone else had somehow done.
Two women sat and drank the lagers they
Were drinking when I'd gone. If anyone
Knew I was there, or had been, or might stay,
They didn't show it. *Good night*, I almost said,
Went out to find the rain had stopped, walked back
To my hotel, and felt the night, tall, black,
Above tall roofs. And Mr Cooper dead.

The Boys

Six of them climbed aboard,
None of them twenty yet,
At a station up the line:
Flannel shirts rimmed with sweat,
Boots bulled to outrageous shine,
Box-pleats stiff as a board.

Pinkly, smelling of Bass,
They lounged on the blue moquette
And rubbed their blanco off.
One told of where to get
The best crumpet. A cough
From the corner. One wrote on the glass

A word in common use.
The others stirred and jeered.
Reveille was idled through
Till the next station appeared,
And the six of them all threw
Their Weights on the floor. Excuse

For a laugh on the platform. Then
We rattled and moved away,
The boys only just through the door.
It was near the end of the day.
Two slept. One farted and swore,
And went on about his women.

Three hours we had watched this lot,
All of us family men,
Responsible, set in our ways.

I looked at my paper again:
Another H-test. There are days
You wonder whether you're not

Out of touch, old hat, gone stale.
I remembered my twenty-first
In the NAAFI, laid out cold.
Then one of them blew and burst
A bag; and one of the old
Told them to stow it. The pale

Lights of the city came near.
We drew in and stopped. The six
Bundled their kit and ran.
'A good belting would sort out their tricks,'
Said my neighbour, a well-spoken man.
'Yes, but . . .' But he didn't hear.

The Fly

The fly's sick whining buzz
Appals me as I sit
Alone and quietly,
Reading and hearing it
Banging against the pane,
Bruised, falling, then again
Starting his lariat tour
Round and round my head
Ceiling to wall to floor.

But I equip myself
To send him on his way,
Newspaper clutched in hand
Vigilant, since he may
Settle, shut off his shriek
And lie there mild and weak
Who thirty seconds ago
Drove air and ears mad
With shunting to and fro.

And I shall not pretend
To any well of pity
Flowing at such a death.
The blow is quick. Maybe
The Hindu's moved to tears
But not a hundred years
Of brooding could convince
My reason that this fly
Has rights which might prevent
My choosing that he die.

And yet I know the weight
Of small deaths weighs me down,
That life (whatever that is)
Is holy: that I drown
In air which stinks of death
And that each unthought breath
Takes life from some brief life,
And every step treads under
Some fragments still alive.
The fly screams to the thunder.

Death troubles me more rarely
Than when, at seventeen,
I looked at Chatterton
And thought what it might mean.
I know my children sleep
Sound in the peace they keep.
And then, suddenly calm,
The fly rests on the wall
Where he lies still, and I
Strike once. And that is all.

Night Thoughts

Darker than eyes shut in a darkened room,
Colder than coldest hours before the dawn,
My nightmare body leaves its bed to walk
Across the unseen lawn
Where apples nudge my feet. They force a shout
Inside my throat which, struggling, can't get out.

I am awake. The dream is over now.
No one is in the garden, nor has been.
You lie beside me while I count the things
Tomorrow will begin
In idleness, omission or false choice,
In lack of purpose or uncertain voice.

You sleep, and in the dark I hear you breathe
Through certainties, responsibilities.
Sometimes you tell me of your own strange dreams.
Mine are banalities,
Trudging down trodden paths to find a heap
Of fragments unromanticized by sleep.

Letters unwritten: papers on my desk:
Money: my age: things I would not have said
Given another minute to decide.
I stifle in my bed,
Searching for other names to call it by,
This blankness which comes down so finally.

But names are nothing, dreams are nothing, when
The day unrolls itself from second sleep.
Reluctantly, I wake: shave: choose a tie.
These daily things are cheap,
The small wage paid to keep my nightmares small:
Trivial, dull: not terrible at all.

At Birth

Come from a distant country,
Bundle of flesh, of blood,
Demanding painful entry,
Expecting little good:
There is no going back
Among those thickets where
Both night and day are black
And blood's the same as air.

Strangely you come to meet us,
Stained, mottled, as if dead:
You bridge the dark hiatus
Through which your body slid
Across a span of muscle,
A breadth my hand can span.
The gorged and brimming vessel
Flows over, and is man.

Dear daughter, as I watched you
Come crumpled from the womb,
And sweating hands had fetched you
Into this world, the room
Opened before your coming
Like water struck from rocks
And echoed with your crying
Your living paradox.

Sick Child

Lit by the small night-light you lie
And look through swollen eyes at me:
Vulnerable, sleepless, try
To stare through a blank misery,
And now that boisterous creature I
Have known so often shrinks to this
Wan ghost unsweetened by a kiss.

Shaken with retching, bewildered by
The virus curdling milk and food,
You do not scream in fear, or cry.
Tears are another thing, a mood
Given an image, infancy
Making permitted show of force,
Boredom, or sudden pain. The source

Of this still vacancy's elsewhere.
Like my sick dog, ten years ago,
Who skulked away to some far lair
With poison in her blood: you know
Her gentleness, her clouded stare,
Pluck blankets as she scratched the ground.
She made, and you now make, no sound.

The rank smell shrouds you like a sheet.
Tomorrow we must let crisp air
Blow through the room and make it sweet,
Making all new. I touch your hair,
Damp where the forehead sweats, and meet –
Here by the door, as I leave you –
A cold, quiet wind, chilling me through.

White Snow

'White snow', my daughter says, and sees
For the first time the lawn, the trees,
Loaded with this superfluous stuff.
Two words suffice to make facts sure
To her, whose mental furniture
Needs only words to say enough.

Perhaps by next year she'll forget
What she today saw delicate
On every blade of grass and stone;
Yet will she recognize those two
Syllables, and see them through
Eyes which remain when snow has gone?

Season by season, she will learn
The names when seeds sprout, leaves turn,
And every change is commonplace.
She will bear snowfalls in the mind,
Know wretchedness of rain and wind,
With the same eyes in a different face.

My wish for her, who held by me
Looks out now on this mystery
Which she has solved with words of mine,
Is that she may learn to know
That in her words for the white snow
Change and permanence combine –
The snow melted, the trees green,
Sure words for hurts not suffered yet, nor seen.

Scars

How, after thirty years of not
Much daring wildness or bad luck,
Do I have so many? No one shot
At me from rooftops, ran me down,
Used me for bayonet practice. Stuck
In small remembered moments, they
Mark even smaller wounds: yet have grown
As I have, to this very day.

The palm of my right hand, scraped raw
By ash and gravel, takes me to
Myself at seventeen: I saw
The athlete had some praise I lacked,
And so I ran for the House. I grew
Hearty and keen. And then one day
I slipped at relay-practice, cracked
My wrist and tore the flesh away.

A bit of travel, too; one thigh
Grazed by stony reefs at sea
Off Libya, swimming: and by
My left wrist, where a window fell
At thirteen in Vermont, I see
A quarter of an inch of white.
A doctor's room in Muswell Hill
Made one of them. A certain light

Shows up one eyebrow ruffled where
A beer glass hit it, up in Leeds –
My only brawl. The bristly hair
At the tip of my chin is sparse because

At nine I fell off a chair. It bleeds
Still, if I close my eyes. Yet not
One rates my passport; minor flaws,
So minor that they show me what

A whole half lifetime did not wound.
There is just one I can't explain:
A thin curved band which goes half round
My little finger, like a ring.
It must have hurt, and yet the pain
Means nothing to me: like the scars
I've never worn, like suffering
Not named in small particulars.

At Enoshima

Level and grey, the sea moves from the east
Carrying fish-heads, cartons, broken glass:
Here a rice barrel bursts out of its staves,
Chicken-bones crunch under as I pass.
The holy island does without a priest
But catches tourists after souvenirs,
So picnic litter sprawls in with the waves
To leave a scurf along this stretch of sand,
Cast-offs and shiftings of the shifting land.

And it is here, along that wavering path
Of plastic lemonade jars, bottles, straws,
I find this other souvenir of Japan,
Swept in by tides to join the common shore's
Museum of rejection: a thin lath,
A pointed stake, a spar of wood, a grave
Not made of lasting stuff, to mark a man
Whose name I cannot read, an age and date
I puzzle out like an illiterate.

He died two months ago, in March. It's just
Those characters I know. The flowing brush
Moves elegantly on, leaves me behind
To dumbly feel the holy island crush
That body, now anonymous, to dust.
Whatever else he was I do not know,
Except his dying left for me to find
His cheap memorial. Ignorant, foreign, I
See nothing but this wood, this mystery.

Manhood End

At Manhood End the older dead lie thick
Together by the churchyard's eastern wall.
The sexton sweated out with spade and pick
And moved turf, clay, bones, gravestones, to make room
For later comers, those whose burial
Was still far off, but who would need a tomb.

Among the pebbles, in the molehills' loam,
Turned thighbone up, and skull: whatever frail
Relic was left was given a new home,
Close to the wood and farther from the sea.
Couch-grass grew stronger here and, with the pale
Toadstools and puffballs, masked that vacancy.

In April, on a day when rain and sun
Had stripped all distances to clarity,
I stood there by the chapel, and saw one
Lean heron rising on enormous wings
Across the silted harbour towards the sea.
Dead flowers at my feet: but no one brings

Flowers to those shifted bodies. The thin flies,
First flies of spring, stirred by the rain-butt. Names
Stared at me out of moss, the legacies
Of parents to their children: *Lucy, Ann,*
Names I have given, which a father claims
Because they mean something that he began.

Cool in the chapel of St Wilfred, I
Knelt by the Saxon wall and bowed my head,
Shutting my eyes: till looking up to high

Above the pews, I saw a monument,
A sixteenth-century carving, with the dead
Husband and wife kneeling together, meant

For piety and remembrance. But on their right
I grasped with sudden shock a scene less pure –
A naked woman, arms bound back and tight,
And breasts thrust forward to be gnawed by great
Pincers two men held out. I left, unsure
Of what that emblem meant: and towards the gate

The small mounds of the overcrowded dead
Shrank in the sun. The eastern wall seemed built
Of darker stone. I lay: and by my head
A starling with its neck snapped: nestling there,
A thrush's egg with yolk and white half spilt,
And one chafed bone a molehill had laid bare.

Frail pictures of the world at Manhood End –
How we are shifted, smashed, how stones display
The names and passions that we cannot mend.
The lych-gate stood and showed me, and I felt
The pebbles teach my feet. I walked away,
My head full of the smell my nostrils smelt.

Leavings

I

Emptying the teapot out
Into the drain, I catch sight
Suddenly of flies at work
On some rubbish by the back
Of the shed, and standing there
Smell the small corruption where
A fishbone makes its measured path
Into the leaves, into the earth.

II

Under the raspberry canes I prod to light
Two Roman sherds, a glint of Roman glass,
A bit of bellarmine, some stoneware scraps,
And searching on might find the rougher wares,
Friable, gritty, Saxon: porous stuff
That lets the rain leak through, the dew absorb,
Frost craze and crack. *Frango*, I break, becomes
Fragment, the broken pieces to be joined
To give a date to everything we own.

III

The little duchess, aged four hundred, stirs
To feel the instruments break through the lead.
Troy stands on the nine layers of its filth
And I tread out another cigarette.

IV

Compost of feasts and leavings, thick
Layer after layer of scourings, peelings, rinds,
Bone pressed on potsherd, fish-head sieved to dust,
And in the spoil-heaps goes the fly, the quick
Mouse with her pink brood, and the maggot, slow
To render down the fat. Trash, husk, and rust,
Grass sickled, scythed, and mown, hedge-clippings, leaves,
Wet infiltrations, skins and rags of skins,
Humus of twigs and insects, skeletons
Of petals.
       Stale loaves and fishes so divided out
They feed five thousand trees, five million roots.

V

    Pipes void it to the sea,
    The Thames chokes on its way.
    We live on what we spend,
    Are spent, are lived upon.
    Nothing has an end.
    The compost is my son,
    My daughter breeds the dust,
    We become ash, air,
    Water, earth, the past
    Our daughters' sons share.

The Pond

With nets and kitchen sieves they raid the pond,
Chasing the minnows into bursts of mud,
Scooping and chopping, raking up frond after frond
Of swollen weed after a week of flood.

Thirty or forty minnows bob and flash
In every jam-jar hoarded on the edge,
While the shrill children with each ill-aimed splash
Haul out another dozen as they dredge.

Choked to its banks, the pond spills out its store
Of frantic life. Nothing can drain it dry
Of what it breeds: it breeds so effortlessly
Theft seems to leave it richer than before.

The nostrils snuff its rank bouquet – how warm,
How lavish, foul and indiscriminate, fat
With insolent appetite and thirst, so that
The stomach almost heaves to see it swarm.

But trapped in glass the minnows flail and fall,
Sink, with upended bellies showing white.
After an hour I look and see that all
But four or five have died. The greenish light

Ripples to stillness, while the children bend
To spoon the corpses out, matter-of-fact,
Absorbed: as if creation's prodigal act
Shrank to this empty jam-jar in the end.

Lesson

In the big stockyards, where pigs, cows and sheep
Stumble towards the steady punch that beats
All sense out of a body with one blow,
Certain old beasts are trained to lead the rest
And where they go the young ones meekly go.

Week after week these veterans show the way,
Then, turned back just in time, are led themselves
Back to the pens where their initiates wait.
The young must cram all knowledge in one day,
But the old who lead live on and educate.

Two Faces

One gets inured to having the wrong face.
For years I thought it soft, too pink and young
To match that shrewd, mature, and self-possessed
Person behind it. In a forced grimace
I saw all that I should have been, the strong
Line linking nose to mouth, the net of care
Fixed by the concentration of the eyes.
Such marks upon the lineaments expressed
Things that I wanted most, but would not dare,
Prevented by the innocence I despised.

Yet now, this morning, as I change a blade,
Look up and clear the glass, I recognize
Some parody of that scored, experienced man.
But this one, as I take it, seems afraid
Of what he sees, is hesitant, with his eyes
Shifting away from something at my back.
No, this is not the one I recognized
Proleptically in mirrors; neither can
He any longer see what firm lines track
Back to that innocence he once despised.

The Stones of Emptiness

Isaiah 34[11]

Eroded slabs, collapsed and weathered tables,
Porous and pocked limestone, rubble of schist:
They are the real blocks where the real foot stumbles,
Boulders where lizards move like Medusa's prey
Freed from their stone trance. Here the stone-eyed exist
Among pebbles, fossil-bearing images
Glaring their life-in-death in the blinding day.
At the dark cave's mouth they stand like effigies.

They define the void. They assert
How vast the distances are, featureless, bare.
Their absence creates the extremest kind of desert,
A sea of sand. They are to the desolate earth
What a single hawk is to the desolate air.
And suddenly here, grouped in a circle
In the middle of nowhere, they form a hearth
Round a fire long since dead, built by an unknown people.

The soil profitless under their strewn acres,
Even so they harbour in their ungenerous shade
Flowers as delicate as they themselves are fierce.
Scorpions entrench under them, flat as dry leaves.
In parched wadi beds, coagulate in a blockade
Against all but a man on foot, who, waterless
And far from home, stumbles as he perceives
Only that line of confusion, the stones of emptiness.

Buzzards Above Cyrene

Alone or in wheeling squadrons of dozens, they move
High above the escarpment, drift to the plain below,
The sun with a certain light obscuring their wings
So that they vanish to narrowed points of darkness
Only to swing away a moment later
Becoming spread sails, gold, brown, distinct and huge
Over tombs, junipers, red stones, red dust
Caught in a still and windless stretch of blue.
But more than that, they impose a scale by which
You measure these golden ruins, these hanging gardens of
    fossils,
These clear imperial edicts and pieties
Cluttering the ledges with magnificence,
All narrowed to points of light in an unwinking eye
For which, fathoms down, a mouse freezes still, a lizard
Flashes, a dung beetle labours through dry thorns,
Regarded, moved over like a dowser's twig,
To twitch then, jerk down, pounce, finding nothing there
But these poor small spoils, these puny snacks and beakfuls
Littered among ruins, squalid among remains,
Ravaged, scavenged, picked clean among pink blooms.

ANTHONY THWAITE

Arabic Script

Like a spider through ink, someone says, mocking: see it
Blurred on the news-sheets or in neon lights
And it suggests an infinitely plastic, feminine
Syllabary, all the diacritical dots and dashes
Swimming together like a shoal of minnows,
Purposive yet wayward, a wavering measure
Danced over meaning, obscuring vowels and breath.
But at Sidi Kreibish, among the tombs,
Where skulls lodge in the cactus roots,
The pink claws breaking headstone, cornerstone,
Each fleshy tip thrusting to reach the light,
Each spine a hispid needle, you see the stern
Edge of the language, Kufic, like a scimitar
Curved in a lash, a flash of consonants
Such as swung out of Medina that day
On the long flog west, across ruins and flaccid colonials,
A swirl of black flags, white crescents, a language of swords.

Silphium

Thick-rooted and thick-stemmed,
Its tail embracing its stem,
Its flower-globes gathered in knots,
Now dead as the dodo,
The mastodon and the quagga,
Commemorated on coins
And in hideous Fascist fountains,
It stands as panacea
For whatever ill you choose,
Since no one living has seen it
Cure dropsy, warts, or gripe,
Flavoured a stew with it,
Or slipped it with a wink
As aphrodisiacal bait.
But there it all is in the books,
Theophrastus, Strabo, Pliny,
Fetching its weight in silver
In the market at Cyrene,
Kept in the state treasury,
Sold to equip the army
By Caesar, sent to Nero
As a rare imperial prize.
Where has it gone? The carious
Teeth of the camel, perhaps,
Have munched it away, or the goat
Scouring the dry pastures.
But I cannot credit the tough
Uncomplicated grasp
Of a plant loosening hold on life
Completely: I imagine a small
Hidden cleft in the worn rock,

Shaded by prickly pear,
Nervously footed by gecko,
Where, thick-rooted and thick-stemmed,
Its tail embracing its stem,
Those flower-globes gather in knots,
That solitary stance
Eluding the oil-prospectors,
The antiquaries, the shepherds,
Who are searching for something else
And need no panacea.

Ali Ben Shufti

You want coins? Roman? Greek? Nice vase? Head of god,
    goddess?
Look, shufti here, very cheap. Two piastres? You joke.

I poke among fallen stones, molehills, the spoil
Left by the archaeologists and carelessly sieved.
I am not above ferreting out a small piece
From the foreman's basket when his back is turned.
One or two of my choicer things were acquired
During what the museum labels call 'the disturbances
Of 1941': you may call it loot,
But I keep no records of who my vendors were –
Goatherds, Johnnies in berets, Neapolitan conscripts
Hot foot out of trouble, dropping a keepsake or two.
I know a good thing, I keep a quiet ear open when
The college bodysnatchers arrive from Chicago,
Florence, Oxford, discussing periods
And measuring everything. I've even done business with
    them:
You will find my anonymous presence in the excavation
    reports
When you get to 'Finds Locally Purchased'. Without a B.A. –
And unable to read or write – I can date and price
Any of this rubbish. Here, from my droll pantaloons
That sag in the seat, amusing you no end,
I fetch out Tanagra heads, blue Roman beads,
A Greek lamp, bronze from Byzantium,
A silver stater faced with the head of Zeus.
I know three dozen words of English, enough French
To settle a purchase, and enough Italian
To convince the austere *dottore* he's made a bargain.

As for the past, it means nothing to me but this:
A time when things were made to keep me alive.
You are the ones who go on about it: I survive
By scratching it out with my fingers. I make you laugh
By being obsequious, roguish, battered, in fact
What you like to think of as a typical Arab.
Well, Amr Ibn el-As passed this way
Some thirteen hundred years ago, and we stayed.
I pick over what he didn't smash, and you
Pay for the leavings. That is enough for me.
You take them away and put them on your shelves
And for fifty piastres I give you a past to belong to.

Butterflies in the Desert

Thrown together like leaves, but in a land
Where no leaves fall and trees wither to scrub,
Raised like the dust but fleshed as no dust is,
They impale themselves like martyrs on the glass,
Leaving their yellow stigmata. A hundred miles
And they form a screen between us and the sparse world.
At the end of the journey we see the juggernaut
Triumphant under their flattened wings, crushed fluids.
Innocent power destroys innocent power.
But who wins, when their bloody acid eats through chrome?
In the competition for martyrs, Donatus won,
But the stout churches of his heresy now stand
Ruined, emptied of virtue, choked with innocent sand.

At Asqefar

At Asqefar the German helmet
Rests like a scarecrow's bonnet
On a bare branch.
The shreds of coarse grey duffel
Hang round the gap a rifle
Left in a shallow trench.

'Much blood', said the shepherd,
Gesturing with his head
Towards the bald hillside.
A spent cartridge nestles
Among the dry thistles.
Blood long since dried.

Strange and remote, almost,
As these old figures traced
In Asqefar's cave:
There, pictured in red clay,
Odysseus comes back from Troy
Near the German's grave.

Twenty-five years since the battle
Plucked up the sand and let it settle
On the German soldier.
Far away now the living, the dead,
Disarmed, unhelmeted,
At Troy, at Asqefar.

Qasīda on the Track to Msus

Towards sundown we came out of the valley
Along that track
Not knowing then where it led to, when we saw
The stone circles, the heaped cairns of stone, the stones
Arranged like coracles on the dry slopes.
The brown hills were empty. Only a buzzard
Stood in the sky, perceiving its territory.

Stopping, we knew the place for an encampment
Or what remained of one: the litter of pots,
The broken shafts of ploughs, battered tin bowls,
Sickles and shears rusting, the chattels of the living.
But there were the dead too, in those stone enclosures
Laid into sand below tattered banners, marked with a stone
At head and foot. For them the tents had moved on,
The blanketed camels, the donkeys heaped high
With panniers and vessels for water. And for us too:
We had passed beyond the wells and the fresh springs
Where the goats shuffled in black congregations,
Beyond even the last dry Roman cistern before Msus
At the end of a track we never intended to take.
Behind us, the barking of dogs and the wind from the sea,
Neither concerned with us nor the way south:
In front, the steppes of gazelles and scorpions
To be hunted or burned, for those who might venture
Further into that camouflage.

But, because it was sundown, we slept there and lay
Hearing the wind, watching the rising moon
Above stars falling like snow through constellations
We could not name. At dawn, we turned back

Into the accustomed valley, a settled place,
Going between tents and herds, yelped at by dogs,
Watched by threshers and gleaners, moving among men.

And still on that hillside the ragged flags fret
Over the abandoned implements and stones,
And now I shall never reach Msus,
Having turned back to the easy valley, while those
Who were not left behind rode, I suppose, south
To some name on the map I might just recognize,
Or a day's ride beyond to a name I do not know.

The Letters of Synesius

Letter III

I would rather live a stranger among strangers.

The slopes below the cave are thick with flints.
Here they kept ammunition in the war,
And now tether a bullock to a post
Under the eaves of rock.
                        Places of the mind only,
Unvisited oases, tracks marked
On unreliable maps by engineers
Who saw the landscape from two thousand feet.

So it might be a god would wander
Over the landscape deserted by his people,
Looking for evidence that once they loved him.
Now they are gone. Delicate microliths
Like snowflakes litter the dry slopes, among thorns.

I am writing to you to talk about emptiness
Because this is empty country, 'where ruins flourish'.

At first you are frightened of dogs, their distant barks
Coming closer across the strewn, ungrateful rock,
And perhaps you pick up stones to shy them away.
You are right, you trespass. Take tea with them, learn the
    words
For 'please' and 'thank you', bark in Arabic,
Or whatever language is current at the time:
Try Berber, Greek, Latin, Turkish, Italian,
Compounds of these, gibbering dialects –

You will still sweat with fear, ducking down for stones
Which, it may be, are tools fashioned by men
Without a language.
                    To call a man a dog
Is an insult in many languages, but not to dogs.
They sniff the high octane at Benina as the planes take off,
Watching the passengers who have an hour
Between London and Nairobi, the pale transients.
Their yellow fur bristles, they yawn and snap.
At Hagfet er-Rejma they patrol the tents,
Watching me glean the slopes for polished flakes.
My pockets are full, my hands are empty.
Look, dogs, how empty. This landscape is yours, not mine.

Letter VII

I am breathing an air tainted by the decay of dead bodies.
I am waiting to undergo myself the same lot that has befallen
so many others.

Lethe, rock fissure, dark water, warm
Breath of white mist on drifting scum, not moving
Unless a white shape moves from rock to rock.
Nostrils drink steam, the air has shapes, can be touched,
Assumes phantoms. Drink here, drink, the brackish taste
On the roof of the mouth, closed with a green coin.
I am ready to descend, to enter the cave's mouth,
To put on the mist's habit, boarding the frail
Craft that has come to claim me.
                                In 1938
The Lido at Lethe was opened to the public
And a poem by d'Annunzio was unveiled
Limned on a carefully ruined stele. Balbo
Offered full citizenship to all who filled in
The necessary forms. Electric cables

Illuminated the forgetful waters and
Two wrought-iron gates guarded oblivion.
Bertolo Giannoni at about this time
Managed to reach the grotto's far wall
And scratched his name in letters a metre high.
Perhaps by some irony he was one of those
Crushed by the tank-tracks of Keith Douglas's troop
On the way through to Agheila and Tripoli.
Bertolo survives on the wall, having drunk the waters.

The filth of pigeons, two fig trees' silver leaves,
Roots splayed from rock channels. Persephone in fossils.
He threw the switch and the sixty-watt bulbs flashed on
Too feebly to desecrate the pre-electric dark.
I walked on duck-boards over the breathing lake.
The mist came walking towards me.

                              Death is a mystery
Not needing these adventitious theatricals.
In the ancient darkness the eirenic shades sleep,
Forgetting Lethe, rock fissure, dark water, warm breath.

Letter IX

*Brought up outside the pale of the Church, and having
received an alien training, I grasped at the altars of God.*

The Dalmatians have landed their advance party
And the billeting-officer is hard at work.
I can now administer the Mass in Serbo-Croat
But the congregation is thin. I carry Christ
Like a burden on my tongue. Andronicus –
From tunny fisher's perch to governor's chariot –
Is excommunicated, but runs giddy still.
My bow sprouts mould in the yard, I have given away
My dogs, my saddle.

                       Once there was philosophy

But how can that clear stream run when I spend my days
Adjudicating ruridecanal tiffs at Hydrax or Darnis,
Squabbles about copes or the laying on of hands?
Hypatia, remember the hush in the lecture-room
When you entered serenely with your astrolabe
And began to enunciate truths?
                    Tonight at five
A conversation-lesson with the Praetor, whose Greek
Would not fill a sardine. Yes, I am peevish.
You may say it is the climate or the place or my time of life –
But I carry a burden that was given to me
Which I do not understand. Somewhere, God's plan
Is hidden in monoliths or a wafer of bread.
His purpose obscurely works through those Slavs on the hill
As I offer his flesh and blood. Neither Gentile nor Jew
In that Kingdom. So I puzzle it out, till I hear
A knock at my study door. Come in, Praetor, come.

Letter XII

*I am a minister of God, and perchance I must complete my
service by offering up my life. God will not in any
case overlook the altar, bloodless, though stained by
the blood of a priest.*

I have reached the end. I shall write to you no more.
Dies irae is come. See the hole in heaven
The tribesmen of Cyrene showed to Battus.
I cling to the church's pillars. These are the Kingdom's last
   days.
Here are the stoups of holy water, here
The table of sacrifice. The victim is also here.

Set sail for Jedda or Jerusalem,
The miracles are due. Here is a splinter

They say is from the Rood, and here a flag
That has snuffed the air of Mecca. I leave myself
As an unholy relic, to be the dust
Neglected by the seller of souvenirs
Among his lamps, his bronzes, his rubbed coins.
Here by the shore God's altar is made whole,
Unvisited by celebrants, to be restored
By the Department of Antiquities.
Functional concrete (ruddled, grey, and brash)
Marks out what's lacking: marble, granite, wood
The divine interstices.

            I abdicate
Having survived locust, earthquake, death
Of children, failure of crops, murrein of hopes,
And am become that ambassador in bonds
Paul spoke of.

            Now the muezzin calls his first
Exhortation, and the pillars fall.
Darkness is on the Jebel, tongues of flame
Bring ruin, not revelation. See how they lick
The rod of Aaron, Zelten's oily fires
Flaring against the night. The visions come.
The pilgrims have boarded, the pagans are at my throat.
The blood of a Greek is spilt for the blood of a Jew.
Altars are stained, a lamb is dragged by its legs
To bleed at the door of the house.

            Libya,
Image of desolation, the sun's province,
Compound of dust and wind, unmapped acres –
This is the place where Africa begins,
And thus the unknown, vaguer than my conjectures
Of transubstantiation, Trinity,
All those arcana for which, now, I die.

At the Italian Cemetery, Benghazi

Meglior un giorno da leone che
centi anni da pecora.

Mussolini

The old rhetoric inflated beyond rigour,
The Roman virtues in a cloud of sand
Blown to a mirage, detonate and roar
Like the lion, extinct since Balbo pressed the trigger
In 1936, far in the south. Here
A place of cypresses, a little Italy
Grazed by the desert wind, an enclave
For the dead, for a dead colony.
Among them all, not one unpolluted grave.
Mare Nostrum is someone else's sea.

The Mediterranean was to be a lake
Round which the *imperium* flourished. There came
Boatloads of dialects, music, priests,
A whole army: bushels of grain,
Cattle, tractors: archaeologists to make
The past justify the present. *Hang thirty a day*
And resistance will stop. Subdue and civilize.
The sun has flaked the neat stucco away.
Sepia fades from Cesare's, from Fabbro's eyes.
The sheep are slaughtered, the lion would not stay.

White villages were built, made ready, named
Heroically or nostalgically:
D'Annunzio, Savoia, Maddalena.
Rebels were strangled, nomads gaoled and tamed.
Dutiful bells rang across jebel and plain,
'Ave Marias' drowning the muezzin's cry.

Calabria, Naples, Sicily put out
Frail shoots into the hot breath of the ghibli.
'Duce, Duce', the parched gullets shout,
Then the bombs fall, the echoes drift and die.

Vulgar memorials, stricken and deluded:
Marble sarcophagi, vain crucifix.
Walking here, why am I now reminded
Puzzlingly of what some cynic said:
Life is a preparation
For something that never happens? The Italian dead
Are gathered under their alien cypresses,
The path gives off its dusty exhalation,
The broken arm of an angel lifts and blesses
The lion-crazed, the shepherdless, one by one.

Augustine at Carthage

No one had told me this was what to expect:
The mouth full of ashes, still warm from the promised feast,
And the slivers of bone hacked from the offered beast
And the dry knot in my gullet not wanting to swallow.
No one told me. Released
From condign ambitions, from words of a worldly text,
I stand on this spit of sand, pointing north from home,
Stale spit sour in my mouth, the devils brought low
In front across tracts of livid disordered foam
And behind across still deserts, unsettlable waste.

Without dignity, without position
Except to keep upright, propped between day and night,
The refugees crowd wanly out of sight:
But I know they are there, unsummoned to the feast,
Without fire, without light,
In attitudes of abandon or contrition.
They have suffered: suffer: the losers, they pay
For their leaders' heresy, the mark of the beast
Branded yesterday, confirmed today
To go on suffering, until proved contrite.

Carthage, you too were brought low, garnished with salt,
A triumph of waste, defaced for your impudence.
I have seen our enemies burned for their vile offence,
Should find it just, should applaud the divinity
That has wrung the due expense
Out of that proven vileness. Scrupulous to a fault,
I measure the given word against the deed
And find the blistered child on its mother's knee
Wrings something out beyond justice: makes me bleed
For something unassurable, for innocence.

But I am committed. I accepted the thorny crown,
The stigma of blood, the word in the desert, the thrall
Banishing all but the doctrine that those who fall
Fall through the truculent will, gone wild and free.
There is no parable
Our Lord told that has set these scruples down
As I would wish them. Committed to this war,
I must accept devout belligerency.
And yet as the desert winds and the waves roar
Across this headland, I pray for some sure call
To deafen our hymns, to rise and drown us all.

Monologue in the Valley of the Kings

I have hidden something in the inner chamber
And sealed the lid of the sarcophagus
And levered a granite boulder against the door
And the debris has covered it so perfectly
That though you walk over it daily you never suspect.

Every day you sweat down that shaft, seeing on the walls
The paintings that convince you I am at home, living there.
But that is a blind alley, a false entrance
Flanked by a room with a few bits of junk
Nicely displayed, conventionally chosen.
The throne is quaint but commonplace, the jewels inferior,
The decorated panels not of the best period,
Though enough is there to satisfy curators.

But the inner chamber enshrines the true essence.
Do not be disappointed when I tell you
You will never find it: the authentic phoenix in gold,
The muslin soaked in herbs from recipes
No one remembers, the intricate ornaments,
And above all the copious literatures inscribed
On ivory and papyrus, the distilled wisdom
Of priests, physicians, poets and gods,
Ensuring my immortality. Though even if you found them
You would look in vain for the key, since all are in cipher
And the key is in my skull.

The key is in my skull. If you found your way
Into this chamber, you would find this last:
My skull. But first you would have to search the others,
My kinsfolk neatly parcelled, twenty-seven of them
Disintegrating in their various ways.
A woman from whose face the spices have pushed away

The delicate flaking skin: a man whose body
Seems dipped in clotted black tar, his head detached:
A hand broken through the cerements, protesting:
Mouths in rigid grins or soundless screams –
A catalogue of declensions.

How, then, do I survive? Gagged in my winding cloths,
The four brown roses withered on my chest
Leaving a purple stain, how am I different
In transcending these little circumstances?
Supposing that with uncustomary skill
You penetrated the chamber, granite, seals,
Dragged out the treasure gloatingly, distinguished
My twenty-seven sorry relatives,
Labelled them, swept and measured everything
Except this one sarcophagus, leaving that
Until the very end: supposing then
You lifted me out carefully under the arc-lamps,
Noting the gold fingernails, the unearthly smell
Of preservation – would you not tremble
At the thought of who this might be? So you would steady
Your hands a moment, like a man taking aim, and lift
The mask.
         But this hypothesis is absurd. I have told you already
You will never find it. Daily you walk about
Over the rubble, peer down the long shaft
That leads nowhere, make your notations, add
Another appendix to your laborious work.
When you die, decently cremated, made proper
By the Registrar of Births and Deaths, given by *The Times*
Your two-inch obituary, I shall perhaps
Have a chance to talk with you. Until then, I hear
Your footsteps over my head as I lie and think
Of what I have hidden here, perfect and safe.

Worm Within

A souvenir from Sicily on the shelf:
A wooden doll carved out of some dark wood,
And crudely carved, for tourists. There it stood
Among the other stuff. Until one night,
Quietly reading to myself, I heard
It speak, or creak – a thin, persistent scratch,
Like the first scrape of a reluctant match,
Or unarticulated word
That made me look for it within myself

As if I talked to myself. But there it was,
Scratching and ticking, an erratic clock
Without a face, something as lifeless as rock
Until its own announcement that it shared
Our life with us. A woodworm, deep inside,
Drilled with its soft mouth through the pitch-stained wood
And like the owl presaging death of good,
Its beak closing as the dynasty died,
It held fear in those infinitesimal jaws.

So – to be practical – we must choose two ways:
Either to have some expert treat the thing
(Trivial, absurd, embarrassing)
Or throw it out, before the infection eats
The doors and floors away: this Trojan horse
In miniature could bring the whole house down,
I think to myself wildly, or a whole town . . .
Why do we do nothing, then, but let its course
Run, ticking, ticking, through our nights and days?

Entry

Died, 1778: Moses Ozier, son of a woman
out of her mind, born in the ozier ground
belonging to Mr Craft.

Christened with scripture, eponymously labelled,
You lie so small and shrunken in the verger's tall
Archaic writing. Born in the low water meadows
Down the end of lawns where you would be unlikely to walk
Supposing you'd ever got that far in life, no Pharaoh's
      daughter
Plucked you out of the bulrushes, for this was Yorkshire
And prophets had stopped being born. Your lunatic mother
Knelt in the rushes and squirmed in her brute pain,
Delivering you up to a damp punishing world
Where the ducks were better off, and the oziers wetly rustled
Sogged down in the marshland owned by Mr Craft.

It's sense to suppose you lasted a few days
And were buried, gratis, in an unmarked hole at the edge
Of the churchyard, the verger being scrupulous
And not wanting your skinny christened bundle of bones
To lie in unhallowed ground.
                              Poor tiny Moses,
Your white face is a blank, anonymous
Like other people's babies. Almost two hundred years
Since you briefly lay by the cold and placid river,
And nothing but nineteen words as memorial.

I hear you cry in the night at the garden's dark edge.